THE REAL STORY:
DEBUNKING HISTORY

THE REAL STORY BEHIND THE WILD WEST

DANIEL R. FAUST

PowerKiDS press.
New York

Published in 2020 by The Rosen Publishing Group, Inc.
29 East 21st Street, New York, NY 10010

First Edition

Editor: Jill Keppeler
Book Design: Reann Nye

Photo Credits: Cover Heritage Images/Hulton Fine Art Collection/Getty Images; p. 5 Rainer Lesniewski/Shutterstock.com; p. 7 (Crockett) Barney Burstein/ Corbis Historical/Getty Images; p. 7 (Boone) Stock Montage/ Archive Photos/Getty Images; p. 7 (Alamo) Sean Pavone/Shutterstock.com; p. 9 (left) Fotosearch/Archive Photos/Getty Images; p. 9 (right) https://en.wikipedia.org/wiki/File:Annie_Oakley_by_Baker%27s_Art_Gallery_c1880s-crop.jpg; p. 11 (left) Transcendental Graphics/Archive Photos/Getty Images; p. 11 (right) Print Collector/Getty Images; p. 12 https://upload.wikimedia.org/wikipedia/commons/7/79/Winchester_1873.jpg; p. 13 RaksyBH/Shutterstock.com; p. 15 (bottom) Mondadori Portfolio/Getty Images; p. 15 (top) Fotomicar/Shutterstock.com; p. 17 De Agostini Picture Library/ De Agostini/Getty Images; p. 19 (top) Underwood Archives/Archive Photos/Getty Images; p. 19 (bottom) Everett Collection/Shutterstock.com; p. 21 (stetson hat) Xtremest/Shutterstock.com; p. 21 (bowler hat) Mega Pixel/Shutterstock.com; p. 21 (bottom) Semisatch/Shutterstock.com; p. 23 DEA PICTURE LIBRARY/ De Agostini/Getty Images; p. 24 https://commons.wikimedia.org/wiki/File:Pony_express_crop.jpg; p. 25 (top) Christophel Fine Art/ Universal Images Group/Getty Images; p. 25 (bottom) https://en.wikipedia.org/wiki/File:Cody-Buffalo-Bill-LOC.jpg; p. 27 Courtesy of the Library of Congress; p. 29 Pete Ryan/National Geographic/Getty Images.

Cataloging-in-Publication Data

Names: Faust, Daniel R.
Title: The real story behind the Wild West / Daniel R. Faust.
Description: New York : PowerKids Press, 2020. | Series: The real story: debunking history | Includes glossary and index.
Identifiers: ISBN 9781538344682 (pbk.) | ISBN 9781538343463 (library bound) | ISBN 9781538344699 (6 pack)
Subjects: LCSH: West (U.S.)–History–Juvenile literature. | Frontier and pioneer life–West (U.S.)–Juvenile literature.
Classification: LCC F591.F38 2020 | DDC 978–dc23

Manufactured in the United States of America

CPSIA Compliance Information: Batch #CSPK19. For Further Information contact Rosen Publishing, New York, New York at 1-800-237-9932

CONTENTS

GO WEST!

Almost as soon as the United States was founded, people wanted to move west and settle the frontier. In 1803, the United States, under President Thomas Jefferson, bought the Louisiana Territory from France. The Louisiana Purchase doubled the size of the United States, and Americans were eager to explore and settle this new land.

People had many reasons to move west. Some were fleeing crowded cities such as New York, Boston, and Philadelphia. Others saw the frontier as a way to reinvent themselves or become rich. Some people thought expanding west was the nation's destiny. People today still love stories of the so-called Wild West, with its cowboys and **outlaws** and brave settlers. But how many of those stories are true—or only partly true?

FACT FINDER

The words "manifest destiny" came to mean the belief that it was the American people's duty to settle across North America, from the Atlantic Ocean to the Pacific.

LOUISIANA PURCHASE TERRITORY

The land the United States gained in the Louisiana Purchase eventually became part of 15 states, including Nebraska, Kansas, North Dakota, and Wyoming.

THE MYTH OF THE AMERICAN WEST

The American West is an important part of American history. Over the years, it also became an important part of the American identity. To many people, westward expansion reflects several key qualities that people want to associate with the American spirit, including strength, courage, and **individualism**. The image of the rugged American taming the Wild West has appeared countless times in books, movies, and advertisements.

Many history books tell us stories about explorers, such as Daniel Boone and David "Davy" Crockett, or tales about the pioneers who left everything they knew behind and traveled into unknown and dangerous territory to settle the American frontier. But these figures are only part of the story. What people think of the Old West is as much myth as reality.

KING OF THE WILD FRONTIER

People picture Davy Crockett as a soldier and outdoorsman—but this wild and free figure was also a politician! Crockett was born in 1786 in Tennessee. He was a scout during the War of 1812 and a member of the Tennessee House of Representatives from 1821 to 1823. Starting in 1827, Crockett served three terms in Congress. The many stories about him made him a folk hero during his life, but later plays, books, TV shows, and movies made him into a legend.

DAVY CROCKETT

DANIEL BOONE

Davy Crockett died at the Battle of the Alamo in 1836. More than 100 years later, in 1954, the Disney company started making TV shows and movies about his legend, making him a popular figure again.

One problem with the myth of the American West is that, like a lot of history, it often only includes one point of view. While both Boone and Crockett made contributions to American history, they both were white men, and much of the history we learn is told from the **perspective** of white men.

Like Boone and Crockett, James Beckwourth was an American outdoorsman. Beckwourth, however, was born into slavery in Virginia. African Americans, including many freed and runaway slaves, played a large role in settling the West. The Native American perspective has also been ignored by many history books. The idea that white settlers had to come to the West and tame the land ignores the fact that countless native tribes lived on that land for thousands of years.

WOMEN OF THE WEST

Men weren't the only ones making a name for themselves in the American West—but like the men, the stories of the women of the Old West often became more famous than the reality. Calamity Jane was a well-known hunter and scout, while Annie Oakley became famous for her sharpshooting skills. Laura Ingalls Wilder grew up on the American frontier and wrote many famous children's books, including *Little House on the Prairie.*

James Beckwourth was born in about 1800. He worked closely with the Crow people of Wyoming and lived with them for a time.

ANNIE OAKLEY

OUTLAWS EVERYWHERE?

Jesse James. Billy the Kid. Butch Cassidy. These are just a few of the outlaws who made a name for themselves robbing banks in the American West—or so the stories say. It's easy to get the impression that the American West was a dangerous, lawless place, with outlaws lurking around every corner. However, these outlaws only rarely robbed banks. Stagecoaches and trains were more likely targets.

Billy the Kid was a real person. Countless songs, movies, and books have all contributed to what people think they know about this legendary outlaw. Legend says that Billy the Kid killed 21 people, one for each year of his life, or even more. That makes for a good story, but evidence suggests that he killed only nine people in his lifetime—still quite a few!

DIME NOVELS

Long before the age of movies and television, one of the most popular forms of entertainment was the dime novel. Sold for 10 cents or less, these cheap paperbacks contained exciting stories of adventure, romance, and danger. Cowboys, mountain men, and outlaws were often the subjects of these books. Many dime novels featured heavily **exaggerated** and fictionalized stories of real people, leading to many of the myths and legends about the American West.

While the Old West could be dangerous, some historians today think it wasn't as violent as movies and books often make it out to be. Dime novels contributed to the image of a violent, lawless place.

BILLY THE KID

THE WAY OF THE GUN

Every cowboy had a six-shooter on his hip—right? There is some truth to the notion that guns were a big part of the Wild West. Many people owned them for defense and hunting, and one model of Winchester rifle actually became known as "the gun that won the West." However, many historians say there were controls on guns even then and there.

As the western frontier became more established, communities began cracking down on the open carrying of firearms. Even Dodge City, Kansas, which had a reputation as one of the wildest frontier cities, posted a sign saying "The carrying of Fire Arms Strictly **Prohibited**" in 1878. In some towns, visitors were expected to leave their guns with the local sheriff while they were there.

WINCHESTER 1873 RIFLE

This replica of Front Street in Dodge City gives visitors a glimpse of what the famous city may have looked like.

HIGH NOON

One of the most iconic moments of many western stories is the shootout. Two rival gunslingers face off in the center of town as the curious and concerned townsfolk look on. We've all seen this play out over and over again in books, movies, and television shows. Were Wild West shootouts as common in reality as they are on film?

The typical Hollywood gunfight was actually quite rare in the American West. There are fairly **accurate** accounts of events such as the gunfight between the Earp brothers and the Clanton-McLaury gang in 1881 and the shootout between "Wild Bill" Hickok and Davis Tutt in 1865. Many times, however, accounts of these gunfights were exaggerated by reporters and dime novels—and sometimes by the participants themselves.

SHOOTOUT BEHIND THE O.K. CORRAL

Brothers Wyatt, Morgan, and Virgil Earp represented the law in the mining town of Tombstone, Arizona. The Clantons and McLaurys were murderers and thieves who lived on a ranch outside of town. The two groups struggled for control of the town. In October 1881, this struggle ended when the Earps and their friend Doc Holliday had a shootout with the Clanton-McLaury gang. However, it didn't take place at the O.K. Corral, but in an empty lot behind the corral.

These kinds of gunfights are popular in movies and at Wild West shows around the country, but they rarely happened in real life.

CIRCLE THE WAGONS!

A popular image associated with the American West is the wagon train. Covered wagons became a symbol of the pioneer spirit. During the late 18th century and most of the 19th century, **caravans** of covered wagons carried settlers and their belongings west along famous routes such as the Santa Fe Trail and the Oregon Trail.

Despite these names, however, the routes that settlers followed were not single, clearly marked trails. As pioneers traveled west, they spread out and tried to find faster and safer trails, until a network of different paths crisscrossed the American West. The journey was not an easy one. Pioneers had to worry about running out of supplies, getting lost, sick, or injured, encountering bad weather, damaging their wagons, and losing their horses and oxen.

FACT FINDER

Some people think of Conestoga wagons when they think of wagon trains. However, the wagons used by pioneers were most often the smaller prairie schooners.

A schooner is a type of ship, and the white covering used on the prairie schooner wagons resembled the sails of a ship.

While the pioneers faced many dangers, the least likely was a Native American attack. The image of the settlers circling their wagons to protect themselves from a war party of angry Indians is more a product of Hollywood than history. It would take far too long to put wagons in a circle in an emergency.

In fact, the Native Americans the pioneers did encounter were more likely to trade with them than attack them. Many early pioneers hired members of local tribes as guides. Many more pioneers died from diseases such as cholera than from Native American attacks. About 400 settlers died from native attacks between 1840 and 1860, while the total number of deaths on the trail was about 20,000. Disease caused most settler deaths on the trail.

FACT FINDER

Many pioneers fell victim to merchants who took advantage of the settlers' fears of running out of food and supplies. Whole sections of the trails were littered with unwanted items such as barrels, clothing, and furniture.

Pioneers would circle their wagons at night. However, they did this to keep their horses and cattle from running away and not to protect themselves from Native American attacks.

COWBOYS AND INDIANS

Perhaps the two groups people think about the most when they think of the American West are the cowboys and the Native Americans. However, a lot of what we know about the American West comes from a certain perspective: White Americans. Much of that perspective is historically **biased**, so it's important that we pay attention to both sides.

The cowboy is an American symbol of rugged independence. The popular notion is that cowboys "tamed the West," making it possible for the United States to expand. However, cowboys weren't an American invention at all. The first cowboys were Mexicans who tended herds of cattle and were called "vaqueros"—which later became the word "buckaroo." When American settlers began moving west, they copied many aspects of the vaqueros' **culture**.

FACT FINDER

Watching American movies, it would be easy to conclude that all cowboys were white. In reality, the men hired by ranchers were a **diverse** group. There were Mexican, Native American, and African American cowboys.

STETSON HAT

BOWLER HAT

The popular image of the American cowboy almost always includes a cowboy, or Stetson, hat. However, while cowboys did wear hats, they often wore other kinds of hats. Especially popular were bowler hats, which are dome-shaped (shaped like half a ball) with a narrow brim.

Since European settlers came to the Americas, Native Americans have been subject to **prejudice**, misunderstandings, and often great violence. A major false belief about Native Americans is that there is a single Native American culture. Many movies, books, and television shows tend to show all Native Americans as tepee-dwelling warriors on horseback, each armed with a bow and arrows and wearing a feathered headdress.

However, there are many very different Native American cultures and languages. There were hundreds of different tribes in North America when Europeans arrived, and each tribe had its own culture. The tribes in the Northeast were different from those in the Southwest, who were different from the tribes of the Great Plains. Even within regions, the tribes were different.

CUSTER'S LAST STAND

The Battle of the Little Bighorn and the deaths of Col. George Custer and his 7th Cavalry led, in part, to the **negative** image many white Americans had of Native Americans. In truth, Custer mishandled much of the battle, which only came about because the U.S. government broke a treaty and refused to remove settlers from Native American land. The government ordered the Native Americans to leave, but many gathered to defy the order, and the U.S. Army moved to attack them.

Conflicts between settlers and Native Americans did happen, and people did die. However, most of the time, it was U.S. military forces fighting Native Americans.

THE PONY EXPRESS

Another common symbol of the American West is the Pony Express. You've probably heard about the brave young men who raced across the West on horseback, delivering important letters and papers to the frontier. That much of the story is true.

The Pony Express was created in 1860. A chain of riders would carry mail almost 2,000 miles between Missouri and California in 10 days, half the time it would have taken a stagecoach. The common image of a rugged man on horseback, rifle in hand to fight off Indian attacks, is far from true. Most riders were teenagers, and they were often quite small, to avoid strain on their horses. If they were armed at all, they'd have a small pistol or knife.

PONY EXPRESS RIDER

FACT FINDER

The Pony Express only lasted 18 months and made fewer than 400 runs before it was replaced by the more reliable telegraph. It was also a financial disappointment.

Buffalo Bill Cody was known for being a big promoter of the Pony Express—but he never actually rode for it!

TRAPPERS AND MOUNTAIN MEN

Long before cowboys, ranchers, and settlers, some of the first white people to explore the American West were the mountain men. Their image may be just as iconic as that of the cowboy. Dressed in fur and leather with a rifle at his side and a knife in his belt, the mountain man was a symbol of courage and individualism. Jim Bridger, one of the most famous mountain men, spoke many languages, including French, Spanish, and many Indian languages.

A lot of what we think we know about these men has been exaggerated and **embellished** by books and movies. Most mountain men were trappers who had been employed by fur companies in the East. Many mountain men also worked as scouts and guides for pioneers and the military.

BUFFALO BILL'S WILD WEST SHOW

For many people in the East, the romanticized stories of the West presented by Buffalo Bill's Wild West Show were all they knew. Buffalo Bill's shows included sharpshooting cowgirls, cowboys performing tricks on horseback, buffalo hunts, and attacks by "unfriendly Indians." Although Buffalo Bill Cody had been a scout and buffalo hunter, he was more interested in entertainment and thrills (and making money) than he was in truth and accuracy.

FACT FINDER

Mountain men played an important role in the settling of the frontier. Many of the trails that later were used by pioneers were first explored and mapped by mountain men.

Like many mountain men, Christopher "Kit" Carson was a fur trapper, wilderness guide, and scout. He was hired as a guide by John C. Frémont, who explored and mapped much of the California and Oregon territory.

GOING FOR GOLD

In January 1848, gold was discovered at Sutter's Mill in California. Within a year, people from throughout the United States were moving to California to try to find gold and get rich. The California gold rush had begun. Once people knew the West contained riches, they began looking for those riches everywhere.

There are many stories and legends about buried treasure and lost mines all over the West. Many of these stories are about hidden loot from bank or train robberies. Some are tales of Native American riches hidden from white men. Stories about secret mines include the Lost Dutchman's Mine in Arizona; the treasure at Victorio Peak, New Mexico; and a mysterious gold mine in the Guadalupe Mountains of west Texas. We may never know if these stories are fact or fiction.

FACT FINDER

The California gold rush of 1849 wasn't the nation's first—or second—gold rush. In 1805, a gold rush started in North Carolina. In 1828, there was another gold rush in Georgia.

The mountains in the western United States have many abandoned mines. It's easy to see why people would be so willing to believe that lost or secret mines were also hidden in them.

AT FACE VALUE

It's easy to assume that everything we read or hear is true. But sometimes, people repeat stories as if they're truth. The Wild West has been a popular topic of movies, books, and TV shows for more than 100 years. While some of the amazing stories are true, many have been exaggerated to make for better fiction.

Often, the history that you've learned has been written from one perspective. That can give you a one-sided view. Instead of taking the stories you've learned at face value, try to find historical sources that show another perspective. Look for the stories of Native Americans and other groups that aren't as represented. You may learn a lot about history and the true story of the Wild West.

GLOSSARY

accurate: Free of mistakes.

biased: Having bias, or a tendency to believe that some people or ideas are better than others.

caravan: A group of people or vehicles (such as cars or wagons) traveling together.

culture: The beliefs and ways of life of a certain group of people.

diverse: Having many different types, forms, or ideas.

embellish: To make something more attractive by adding details or features.

exaggerate: To enlarge something beyond the truth.

individualism: The quality of a person who does things without being concerned about what others will think.

negative: About the real or supposed bad qualities of something or someone.

outlaw: A person who has broken the law and is hiding or running to avoid being caught.

perspective: Point of view.

prejudice: An unfair feeling of dislike for a person or group because of race or religious or political beliefs.

prohibit: To say that something is not allowed.

INDEX

WEBSITES

Due to the changing nature of Internet links, PowerKids Press has developed an online list of websites related to the subject of this book. This site is updated regularly. Please use this link to access the list: www.powerkidslinks.com/debunk/west